The Meaning of Your Dreams:

Making Sense of What You Dream, and Finding Out What They Mean to You and Your Life

Fiona Ashling

Table of contents: what's here

Introduction

I know someone who says she never dreams.

By that, she means that she never remembers her dreams.

She's an educated woman, and she knows that everyone dreams. But try as she might, she can never remember then when she wakes up.

Me, I'm different. I remember them almost every morning. I remember the odd ones, and the ordinary ones. I remember the one's that frighten me, and the ones that puzzle me. I remember scary dreams, and comforting ones.

Dreams are a huge mystery. We normally spend about one third of our lives asleep. We still don't know why we sleep. Sleep isn't the same as rest. If we allow someone to lie down, "resting," but don't allow them to sleep, that person will go nuts and eventually die. But we don't know for sure what sleep does for the body that depriving the body of sleep is so damaging.

But one of the theories is that we sleep because we have to dream. That doesn't give us much more of a clue about the "whys" of what we do every night. But we know that everyone dreams. And many of us remember our dreams, and most of those folks who remember want to know the meaning of our dreams.

That's what this book is about: the meanings of your dreams. I'm not here to give you theories and speculation - I'm here to provide what are thought to be the meanings of the various things and people and events that occur in dreams, and help you figure out how to understand those dreams in the context of your life.

The contents of our dreams are usually in broad categories, and so we'll put our explanations in those broad categories. Each broad section (say, on animals) will be broken down into sub-sections (in the animal section, for example, there will be sections on dogs, bats, bears, etc.)

Chapter One: Animals

BATS

Dreaming of a flying bat means a catastrophe is coming, but not necessarily to the dreamer. Often this catastrophe involves water, such as a drowning or accident.

To dream of a motionless bat often means some illness (serious or not) is coming but again, not necessarily to the dreamer.

If a bat settles on the dreamer, then the dreamer will be the one who suffers from either an illness or injury.

Generally speaking, a dream about bats indicates that a disaster is coming. To give you an idea, a woman once dreamed that she was crossing a field when she heard a loud buzzing sound overhead, and when she looked up, there was a large number of bats above her, whirling round and round in chaos and confusion. Then the bats swooped down, and began swirling round and round her face, but never close enough to touch her, and while they were swirling round her head, she woke up. Obviously, this was a terrifying dream, and she realized something bad was coming, and 2 days later, her sister drowned in a swimming accident.

A man in India who was originally from England wrote about his experiences with bat dreams. He had 2 dreams of bats that led foretold disaster.

In the first one, he dreamed that he was sitting on his bed in his childhood home there in England. In the dream, six bats, one after the other, flew in the window, and after whirling around the room, vanished in the way things sometimes do in dreams. The next day, he got a phone call telling him that his brother had drowned while swimming in the ocean.

Last year, he had another such dream. In the dream, he was riding on the subway in London, near where he grew up. Suddenly, a bat flew past him on the subway, and the rest of the passengers shouted together, "Amazing! A bat!" and the man dreaming woke up actually repeating those words.

The man was so impressed by this odd dream that he made notes about the dream.

Exactly a week later, he received another sad phone call: his father had been hunting, and had fallen to his death down a steep hill.

In dreams referring to motionless bats, one woman told of dreaming that her bed was covered with bats. This woman was particularly terrified of bats, and she woke up immediately after the dream, and her body was covered in sweat.

The next day, she learned that one of her aunts who she particularly loved was seriously ill, and within a week, the aunt was dead.

Another woman dreamed that she saw her youngest sister lying on her back in the grass, apparently asleep, with two bats on her face. In the dream, the woman cried out, and picked up a shovel to knock the bats off, and suddenly the scene changed, and she was digging a grave. She woke up terrified, and two days later her sister was dead from complications of a botched appendectomy.

Another woman wrote that her sister dreamed that a bat settled on her shoulder, and she couldn't get it off. She woke up terrified, and couldn't quit thinking that the dream foretold something terrible. Her fears were sadly correct: shortly after the dream, the sister became severely ill, and died of pneumonia.

BEARS

Bears have always been considered a bad omen in

the world. Even when bears are not threatening, most people are scared of them if they meet them in the wild. Encountering them in a dream is no different.

One young man told me that he dreamed that a huge, shaggy bear with a demonic expression in its little brown eyes had entered his room, and coming to the foot of his bed, stood on its hind legs, and stared at him. Terrified, he he got out of bed, and had almost reached the window, when the bear walked up to him, placed its paws on his shoulders, and breathed on his face. He woke with the memory of the bear's hot breath burning in his brain, and said that his life and behavior were changed from that night. Had he not changed, he would probably have gone to prison.

A homeless woman I once met said that she thought her string of bad luck had started from the bad influences of a dream. "I was working at a Starbucks in Milwaukee at the time," she said, "and beyond liking to spend too much on clothes, I'd never done anything wrong. But one night, I dreamed I was at a dance, and my partner was a bear. He was a good dancer, and I fell in love with him. He told me he'd drive me home, and when we got there, he suddenly kissed me, and I woke up with the memory of his nasty wet mouth on my lips. Try as I could, I couldn't get the dream out of my mind. I kept seeing the bear, whether I was at work or in a restaurant or out biking. My thoughts were always about him, and I got really messed up. I was engaged, but I started arguing with my fiance, and ended up breaking that off that engagement. I got engaged to someone else almost immediately, and broke that off in six months, and was quickly engaged to another guy. I made excuses to show off my new guys to my ex's. I started spending money recklessly, and got in debt, and started embezzling money from my employer, and ended up in prison. And it's all because of that nasty, disgusting bear."

I think these two stories give you an idea about the significance of bear dreams. Bears in a dream are just no good.

BIRDS

Bird dreams are extremely common, and we could write an entire book about them. But since our time is limited, we'll deal with a few of the biggest bird dreams.

Dreaming about canaries is a good sign - usually a sign of money. Either money from an inheritance, a salary increase, or a present.

Dreaming about doves implies good fortune not necessarily related to money - such as recovery from illness, success in work, or success in love.

Dreaming about a cuckoo bird means an unexpected find, for example, finding something of value, or finding something that was lost long ago, and for which the finder had given up hope on.

On the other hand, dreaming about crows is a sign of bad luck, and signifies losses - monetary or otherwise, quarrels and disappointments.

Ducks are a good sign in dreams, portending good fortune, presents, and physical love.

To dream about chickens implies quarrels. To dream about geese indicates new clothing.

Not surprisingly, dreaming about eagles indicates a coming great success, while dreaming of vultures indicates failure or illness.

Magpies, whether a single bird, or a group, mean death. If the birds are in flight, it indicates the death of an acquaintance or friend. If the bird is motionless, it indicates the death of the dreamer.

Dreaming about hawks means that the dreamer is about to make an enemy. Dreaming about owls indicates the breaking of a friendship, breaking off of a serious relationship, serious illness, an accident or death.

Parrots in dreams are foretelling some impending scandal or gossip, while pigeons signify that the dreamer is about to receive presents.

Ravens are a sign of grave misfortunes coming along.

Sparrows signify petty losses and quarrels.

Swallows are a sign of grief at someone's illness, misfortune or death, but are a sure sign of grief of some variety.

Storks mean an approaching birth.

Wrens an approaching engagement or marriage.

These are but a few of the accounts of bird dreams upon which these interpretations are based.

One woman writing from Alabama said, "I'm sure canaries in dreams are a sign of extremely good fortune. Just 2 years ago, I dreamed that a canary had hit my window, and the next day, I received a very generous check from an uncle I'd lost contact with for several years. The night before last, I dreamed of a couple of canaries flying around my bed and singing, and that very day, I got a letter from an attorney, telling me that I'd received an unexpected inheritance.

One girl wrote to say that she likes to dream about ducks. "They mean so much!" she said. "I dreamed of ducks a week ago, and the next day a boy I had always liked kissed me. He'd always been very shy, and I was surprised at that. But duck dreams are always good. When I dreamed about them once before, you'll never guess what I got the next day - a watch I'd always wanted, an unexpected gift from an aunt who had hardly ever given me anything. I'm planning to dream about ducks as often as I can!"

On the other hand, the experience of an elderly woman from Wyoming was not so pleasant. "I dread seeing or dreaming about magpies," she says. "They always indicate a death. I dreamed about three magpies coming in front of me the day before my father died, and I dreamed that a huge magpie flew in the door and perched on my bed, exactly a week before my oldest son died."

Another woman wrote that a close relative died just after the woman dreamed about a large number of magpies flying in her window, and the day before a dog she was very attached to died, she dreamed of two magpies landing on her shoulder, and she could not make them leave.

One man writes about living in a large house in the Boston area, and dreaming that a raven flew down the chimney and pecked him hard three times on his hand. The pecking was so intense that he woke up, and while the room was quiet, and completely dark, he turned on his other side, and suddenly saw a light and looked up and saw a vision of an old hag in the window, and the window was almost thirty feet off the ground. He'd been in that house for several months and hadn't seen or heard anything unusual, and had decided to ignore the rumors of the house being haunted, and decided that the rumors were just that - stupid stories being repeated by ignorant people. Now as he stared at the window, rubbing his eyes to make sure he wasn't asleep, he realized that the rumors were well-founded, and he never slept in that room again. The hag was only visible for a few seconds and when he sat up, it was gone. This man isn't the only one who's dreamed of ravens just before seeing something supernatural.

Another man dreamed of a wren just before he became engaged, and three people wrote to say that they always dream of a wren before hearing about a marriage.

Larks are usually a sign of good news about friends and relatives and happy events in general.

Linnets indicate marriages, while thrushes are a sign of minor illnesses and troubles.

BULLS

Dreaming about being chased by a bull indicates that an accident is coming. These are usually minor problems, such as breaking something, or a minor loss, and not usually anything more serious. One man from Chicago dreamed that he was being chased by a bull down Michigan Avenue there, and the next day, he dropped and broke his cell phone.

In another case, a woman who worked at a restaurant dreamed of a bull chasing her down and street, and tossing her off a bridge, and the next day she dropped a large tray full of dishes at the restaurant.

CATS

Dreaming about a white cat is luck. On the other hand, dreaming about a black cat is either very lucky, or very unlucky. Dreaming about a tabby cat is neutral - neither lucky nor unlucky. Dreaming about a mottled cat ("tortoiseshell") cat is a sign of disaster.

These are some good examples of cat dreams. An English woman wrote that she and her daughters had dreamed about white cats on several occasions, and those dreams were always a sign of astonishing good luck. Her oldest daughter had dreamed of a cat jumping on her shoulder and refusing to leave the night before she got an email telling her that she'd won an academic award. Her second daughter dreamed that she was rowing on a lake that was overcrowded with white cats that were having a great time swimming around her. Every now and then they would climb on board the boat and rub their noses against her, and a day or two later, she received an unexpected invitation to go with a friend on a cruise. "But," she continued, "The most amazing was my own experience, when my husband out of the blue bought me a beautiful coat I'd been admiring. The night before, I had a vivid dream that a big cat was sitting on a couch in my room, and as soon as it saw me, it jumped into the middle of the room, and sank through the floor."

A striking example of a cat dream being followed by misfortune happened to a California woman, whose father lost a fortune in the stock market during the 2009 recession. "Just prior to everything going downhill," she recounts, I dreamed I saw a tortoiseshell cat on the mantel in my living room. Later on during the same time period, my husband lost a lot of money when a real estate development he was building went bust. Shortly before that, I dreamed I was bitten by another tortoiseshell cat." Not surprisingly, that woman dreads seeing a mottled cat in her dreams.

Many have found dreams of black cats to be very unlucky. In one instance, just before a bad car accident, a man dreamed that a huge black cat followed him out of doors, and when he tried to make it go away, the animal scratched him. The same man dreamed that a black cat had come running out of the woods near his home, and scratched his hand. Following that dream, his eye was injured in an accident. Another time, he dreamed that a black cat had knocked a glass of dark wine on a new suit, completely ruining it. Shortly after that, a series of delays made him miss a flight that was extremely important for him to catch.

COWS

Dreaming about cows appears to indicate good luck in general, and to especially foretell unexpected visits from friends. One woman I know dreamed of cows just before she got a call from a long-distance friend who was unexpectedly in town, and wanted to get together.

CROCODILES

Dreaming about crocodiles is a warning of danger from drowning or other water mishaps or danger from lightning. A dream about a crocodile may also be a sign of sorrow at the loss of a friend.

DEER

Dreams about deer usually precede trouble with the eyes, missing a plane flight or other transportation problems, or other petty annoyances.

DOGS

Dreaming about dogs is a pretty general category, and most people have dreamed about dogs many times. But since there are many breeds of dogs and each breed conveys a different meaning, we can only talk about a few of them for interpretation.

A boarhound in a dream foretells auto accidents or accidents in flight..

A bloodhound may tell of serious financial problems.

A dream about a collie is a sign of breaking up of friendships by deceit or treachery.

A dachshund indicates an unexpected reconciliation with a friend.
A greyhound indicates illnesses or deaths.

A foxhound indicates unexpected news.
A mastiff is a sign of danger from fire.

A Pomeranian indicates danger from theft, such as from robbers, burglars or gangs.

A spaniel is an indication of breaking up of engagements and disappointments in general.

Terriers indicate small successes or arguments.

I've been told of a number of dog dreams, and here are a few of them. These are the ones worth remembering.

One woman I met was from New York, and she dreamed that was walking in the theater district there in Manhattan, and a greyhound jumped from the roof of a nearby house and fell in a heap at her feet. As if this wasn't bad enough, the dream animal suddenly changed into her father. The very next day, out of the blue, she got a call that her Dad had died unexpectedly. She also dreamed, a day or two before the death of her best friend that she was on a flight with two greyhounds seated opposite her.

Another woman told me that shortly before there was a fire in her house, she had an odd dream about a mastiff. The animal entered the room where she was sitting, and suddenly lunged at a rug, and tore it to pieces.

One woman I asked about her dreams told me that she'd been engaged three times and that before each engagement ended, she'd dreamed of a dachshund.

There are even grimmer stories in connection with Pomeranians. One man I met told me he had once dreamed he saw his little boy being frightened by a Pomeranian dog and the next night, his house was burglarized.

Another man, a recent immigrant from south Asia, dreamed that he was alone in a very dark and gloomy church and that a gigantic priest dressed as a priest suddenly appeared in the pulpit and after making a face, he was suddenly transformed into a monstrous Pomeranian dog. The man couldn't remember exactly what happened next, but he thinks it must have been very frightening because he was drenched in sweat and as he woke up he realized that someone was in the room. Not sure if he was still dreaming, he pinched himself, and suddenly someone ran for the door. Other family members heard the commotion, and ran for the room, and caught the man who had hidden in the room - he was a former employee who had been fired for embezzlement, and had planned to rob and kill his former employer. Since the man had dreamed of a Pomeranian on another occasion when he'd been robbed, the man came to the conclusion that dreams about that species of dogs indicated robbery or worse.

DONKEYS

Dreams about donkeys indicates upcoming minor troubles and ailments.

FISH

As with dogs and birds, the subject of dreams about fish is a big one, way too large for me to deal with exhaustively. We'll have to content ourselves with a few selections.

Dreaming about goldfish is very fortunate, and points to inheritances and presents, chiefly involving money.

Whales, on the other hand, indicate impending lawsuits, debts, bankruptcy and other financial difficulties.

Dreaming about sharks predicts death, illness, or an enemy.

To dream about mackerel indicates coming domestic troubles.

Dreaming about herring, pleasures in the form of visits to friends or places of entertainment. Sprats, children's illnesses; pike, quarrels; about flatfish,

misfortunes in some form or other, but seldom
deaths.

Salmon indicate unexpected success, happiness,
presents and the forming of sound friendships.
Minnows and sticklebacks, on the other hand,
portend petty quarrels and disappointments.

Eels are a sign of of disruptions in loving
relationships, nasty problems with enemies and
failures in work.

I've dreamed a lot about fish. I remember once
having a very vivid dream about a shark. I dreamed
I was swimming in a pool near the house where I
was staying, when to my complete surprise, a shark
fin was coming straight toward me. I screamed for
help, and the next minute found myself falling
down a well with the shark, an enormous white
shark coming quickly after me. Coming to the
bottom, I was abruptly in the living room of a
house I'd not visited of thought of for at least

twenty years, and the first thing I saw on the table was the shark's head, its evil eyes fixed on mine with a malicious grin. I woke up terrified, and after tossing and turning for a while, came downstairs to breakfast, and heard of the sudden (and unexpected) death of a close friend.

Another time, a day or two before I heard about the death of an old friend from school, I dreamed I was fishing in a deep pool overgrown with vegetation. The first thing I caught -- or, more accurately, the first thing that caught me, was a monstrous shark, which eventually ate me! I can still see it now, a huge, slimy, blue-backed creature with a glistening white stomach, eyes shining with evil glee at the prospect of a meal, and an enormous, gaping mouth filled with row after row of saw-edged teeth.

I was in the shark's mouth at once, and the next minute was terrifying, as excruciating agony went through me as a thousand knife-like points crushed into my flesh. For seconds after I woke up, I still felt terrible pain in my eyes and ears, and every sensitive part of my body.

One woman told me that the night before she got news that her son had had an unexpected promotion, she dreamed that she saw him standing in a pool of water surrounded by large salmon, rubbing themselves against his legs like a dog would.

Another salmon dream was to the effect that just before the dreamer received a much hoped-for job, he dreamed he was swimming in a stream when he suddenly encountered a huge salmon that leaped out of the water and went rising further and further into the air, until it finally disappeared completely.

It's a common thing to dream about eels and whenever I do, something unpleasant is sure to follow. Either somebody plays a nasty trick on me, or I miss a plane I need to catch, or I get a cold, or am rebuffed in something I need to do.

FOXES

Foxes are so prominent in folklore that we shouldn't be surprised that dreams about foxes are very significant in the case of many people.

Silver foxes in dreams seem to foretell extreme good fortune; black foxes, excessive misfortune; ordinary foxes, a moderate amount of good luck.

One man related a dream he'd had about a fox. "I dreamed," he said, "I was starving to death in the streets of a big city, and had decided that rather than going on in my misery, I'd kill myself by jumping in a deep, brown river that flowed sluggishly by me. Suddenly a white fox came running down the street, and stopping directly in front of me, began to spit out gold coins. I jumped toward the fox, and began to scoop up the coins, and was filling my pockets when I woke up. That day, I won several hundred dollars on a lottery ticket, but I think the fox should get all the credit."

Another man dreamed he was flying a kite when
his coat was pulled violently and turning around,
he saw a white fox run quickly between his legs,
and the fox suddenly changed into the man's uncle.
The creamer was so shocked that he woke up, and
two days later got news that the uncle had died in
his sleep, and the man who had dreamed inherited
the uncle's estate.

FROGS

Dreaming about frogs indicates the coming of
trouble at home, damages, and small losses.

HORSES

Dreaming about white horses foretells good luck of
various kinds. Dreaming about black horses on the
other hand, indicates serious misfortune from
accidents (frequently water accidents), deaths, loss
of money or property, violent arguments, and

break-ups of relationships. Dreaming about a horse with mixed colors is a sign of upcoming travel. Grey horses are a sign of good luck in many ways, such as inheritances, presents, love and work success, etc. Chestnut-colored horses are a sign of dangers of all varieties - fire, water, and other accidents, assaults and illnesses.

If I quoted even half the horse dreams related to me, I could fill a book, so I'll have to be content with just quoting a few.

Just before a violent breakup that ended in divorce, one woman dreamed that she heard a loud neighing outside her house, and looking out, she saw a gigantic black horse with intensely evil eyes, staring up at her. Terrified, she turned to run downstairs to make sure that all the doors were shut, when to her shock and horror, the horse stalked into her room, and savagely rushed at her. She woke up, but was too scared to sleep again until the following morning.

Another interesting dream happened to a man I met from Atlanta. Just before his house caught fire and was almost completely destroyed, he dreamed he was running along a hot and dry country road when a chestnut horse appeared on the scene and began to plunge and snort directly in front of him. Terrified, he stopped, and noticed a greenhouse at the side of the road, and was turning to hide in there, when the horse rushed at him, grabbed him viciously by the back, threw him on the ground, and was about to crush him when he woke up.

A more pleasant dream is one that I had once. Just before I got a long-awaited email telling me that a manuscript I'd written had sold, I dreamed I was walking tired along a dusty road when a beautiful grey horse gently trotted up to me with a kind expression in its fine dark eyes, and told that I was to mount. Not in the least surprised a talking horse, I climbed on its back, and the next minute found myself flying through the air. I couldn't remember the details of how the dream ended, but was left with a pleasant, satisfied feeling when the horse landed me in a field filled with flowers.

Another time I dreamed of a mixed colored horse and it was struggling to get itself out of a swamp, but kept sinking further and further into it and it finally disappeared from sight and nothing was left to mark the spot but a hideous black bubble. This dream happened just before I had to make a sudden (and not pleasant!) business trip.

Chapter 2: INSECTS AND CREEPING THINGS

ANTS

Ants in dreams signify presents.

BEES

Dreaming about bees foretells good luck, often in love and relationships, work or money. I've known of people who dreamed about swarms of bees buzzing around them just before inheriting money. I remember before I became engaged dreaming about bees trying to get into my bedroom window. It was a beautiful sight as their wings and the yellow markings of their bodies flashed and sparkled in the rays of a typical dreamland sun.

BEETLES

Dreaming about black beetles tells of an impending illness, sometimes serious, but other times minor. When I get a bad cold, I often have scary dreams of being visited by swarms of black beetles and roaches.

BUTTERFLIES

Almost all of the time, butterfly dreams are good luck. They usually signify unexpected good luck and happiness.

CATERPILLARS

Dreaming about caterpillars foretells small accidents, such as cuts on fingers, bumps and bruises and minor illnesses and inconveniences such as colds, "stuffiness," and toothache.

CENTIPEDES

Centipede dreams denote loss - often the loss of some pet, other animal, or of a treasure.

DRAGONFLIES

Dreaming about dragonflies portends quarrels, aggravations, and unpleasant tasks.

EARWIGS

Dreaming about earwigs foretells danger from an enemy - an enemy who wants to stab you in the back (metaphorically speaking!) It also signifies danger from scandal and malicious gossip.

GNATS

Dreams about gnats would seem to have special significance to the young -- or the young at heart! That's because gnats in a dream are a sign of kisses.

LADYBUGS

Ladybugs in dreams are lucky, and are a sign of presents - often presents from lovers.

MAGGOTS

Not surprisingly, maggots in dreams are a bad omen, and portend sickness, death, fights, quarrels and losses.

MOTHS

Dreaming about moths is unlucky, and portends disappointments of all kinds, in money matters, love, and work.

SLUGS

Slugs in dreams are a sign of jealousy.

SPIDERS

Dreaming about spiders (with the exception of big, black spiders) is luck, in general. It's a sign of presents and unexpected success in work and business. It's also a sign of travel.

Black spiders, on the other hand, signify danger from drowning and from falls.

SNAILS
Dreaming about snails is a sign of weddings, friends getting back together, and good business success.

WASPS

Wasps in a dream foretells monetary losses, quarrels and disappointments.

WORMS
Dreaming about worms speaks about close and faithful friends and loved ones. They're also a sign

of recovery from illness, and success on the stage and in other acting.

Chapter 3: MORE ANIMALS

KANGAROOS

Kangaroos are a sign of upcoming travel..

LIONS

A dream about lions is a sign of marriage, success of all kinds - in athletics, love, and work, and of an unexpected journey.

Just before a trip to Southeast Asia, planned on the spur of the moment, a woman told me that she had dreamed she was crossing the road in front of her house when she glanced up and saw a lion staring down at her from a window. Terrified for both herself and her children (who were still in the house), she turned to a man nearby to seek his help. Suddenly the lion burst through the window, leaped toward her and began to chase her and she woke up.

I remember dreaming that I was eaten by a lion just before planning to go on an unexpected vacation a few years ago.

LEOPARDS, PUMAS AND PANTHERS

In a dream, these animals signify violent accidents, serious illnesses, and death.

MONKEYS

There are, of course, a large number of monkey species, but generally speaking monkeys in dreams are a sign of quarrels, the breakup of romantic relationships, and lawsuits.

MICE

In some cases, dreams about mice seem to have no meaning in particular, but in others they are a definite sign of illness or even death.

I remember one woman telling me that she had several times dreamed that she was surrounded by mice, and that every time she had this dream, one of her children fell sick.

In another case, a woman dreamed that she was at a dance one night and as she was about to start dancing, a mouse suddenly jumped off her partner's head on to her head and viciously bit off her ear. She woke up hurting from the pain and caught the flu a few days later. The dream was so vivid she couldn't help remembering it, and associating it with illness.

And to cite a case in which a mouse dream foretold death, I met a woman once who dreamed that she saw a line of mice running across her bedroom, and the next morning she got a phone call telling her that her brother had drowned in a sailing accident.

PIGS

Dreaming about pigs is very unlucky, and can mean anything from a slight accident to catastrophic situations.

One woman, just before her youngest child fell down a well, and nearly drowned, dreamed that she saw her son riding up and down on their lawn on a big white pig, and the pig stared at her in an evil manner.

Another man, just before he lost a huge investment in a restaurant venture, dreamed that he saw a herd of white pigs outside his front door, pawing the ground, and crying miserably.

RATS

No matter what their color - white, black, or brown - and no matter whether they are alone or in a group, rats are a sign of sickness, death, and serious problems and misfortunes.

I met a man once who dreamed that his bedroom was full of enormous black rats with gray eyes. The animals raced round and around his bed, and eventually leaped out an open window. The man's son drowned shortly thereafter in a sailing accident.

Another woman I met dreamed that she saw her youngest daughter sitting on the floor playing with a big brown rat that suddenly jumped up at her, tore a ribbon out of her hand, and raced from the room with it. That daughter died shortly after that dream of a sudden and harsh respiratory infection.

SNAKES

Snake dreams are bad luck, and are a sign of problems with enemies, scandal, cruel gossip, and treachery by false friends.

Among the many snake dreams I've heard of, here are some examples.

A woman had formed a close friendship with another woman. The first woman dreamed that she was walking in a garden, when out of a rose an enormous green snake slid out. Terrified, she was about to try to find someone to kill the animal when she saw to her astonishment that the creature had human eyes. Bending down to look more closely, she was amazed to discover that the snake's eyes were the same shape and color as her friend's eyes, but the expression was different: there was an expression of malice and craftiness. Looking more closely, she realized that the snake's "face" was exactly that of her friend. She woke up troubled and learned shortly after this dream that this very friend had done her a great deal of damage by betraying her confidence.

Another such dream is the experience of a man who dreamed he was working on a rock collection in his garden when he was terrified to find a nest of brown snakes that rose on their ends and hissed at him. He tried to move back, only to find himself wedged in by a wall that suddenly sprang up behind him every way he moved. Every means of escape was closed, and wherever he looked, he saw snakes, and the rocks were covered with them. Overcome with fear, he forced himself to wake up, and rather than go to sleep again and risk a repetition of the dream, he turned on a light, and read until morning. Shortly afterward, he was betrayed by a business partner and lost a large investment.

SHEEP

In dreams, sheep indicate the onset of trouble in the form of family feuds and disagreements and quarrels with friends and neighbors.

Apart from experiences with folks I've met, I've found that after dreaming of sheep myself, I've often had to deal with much petty and stupid bickering.

RAMS

Dreaming about rams is a sign of a more violent type of disagreements than do sheep. For example, when I was a boy, prior to an argument (which ended in a fight) with another boy from school, I dreamed I was attacked in a field by a large black ram with red eyes that persistently chased me over hedges and ditches and through a river. Suddenly, in the dream I flew up in the air, but the animal sprang up after me, butting me over and over until I was badly hurt, and finally I woke up.

In later years, before an argument with a nasty lawyer, I dreamed I was fishing in a pond when a gray ram caught me by surprise, butted me in the back, and push me head first into the water, where I was attacked on all sides by slimy, yellow snakes.

STAGS

Stags in dreams are a sign of a serious change in one's life. For example, one young man was trying to make a decision about a serious move for his job. He dreamed that he was walking through a park when a beautiful stag came running up to him and lifted him up with its antlers in a way that wasn't frightening, and didn't hurt him. The stag continued to carry him through some woods and fields and finally brought him to the edge of a vast sea, where it turned into a boat and sailed away.

Another stag dream I was told about involved a man who made a serious career change and dreamed about a white stag that appeared by his bedside, picked him up in its mouth, and sank through the floor to appear in a garden where it became involved in a deadly fight with another stag and after it killed the other stag with its horns it suddenly turned to attack the dreamer, when he awoke.

TIGERS

Dreaming about a tiger is a sign of an oncoming illness, a loss of money, an accident, or disappointment in love. I dreamed I was stalked and pounced on by a white tiger before I was thrown from a bicycle. A night or two before I had a sudden attack of appendicitis in December of 2006, I dreamed a tiger got into the house through an open window, and after it ate my dog, whose screams scared me to death, came running upstairs to attack me. I can't tell you how terrified I was as I heard the animal creeping closer and closer. It was agonizing and I awoke as its hideous, striped head and evil eyes peeked gloatingly in at me through the door.

WOLVES

Dreams about wolves are a sign of big impending trouble, often financial, but sometimes domestic, like in a divorce or separation.

A man told me once about how just before he learned that his wife was having an affair, he dreamed that he saw her riding on the back of a huge gray wolf while a white wolf, which she was petting affectionately trotted by her side.

Another man, just before he lost a fortune in the stock market, dreamed that a pair of black wolves rushed through his yard, howling loudly and biting at everything that came in their way.

Another man told me how, just before a fight with his daughter that led to her running away, he dreamed a big grey wolf leaped into his room and tried to eat him.

ELEPHANTS

Dreams about elephants are a sign of shipwrecks, marriages and births.

TOADS

A toad in a dream foretells vicious acts that will either be done to the dreamer or by the dreamer.

FLIES

Flies in a dream are a sign of an impending illness, often a mental illness, and misfortunes of various kinds.

For example, a man I met in Europe told he that prior to his being hospitalized several times in psychiatric facilities, he continually dreamed that he was surrounded by flies.

Another woman, just before her children became seriously ill, dreamed that her room was filled with flies.

Someone else told me just before she lost her job in an office, she dreamed that she was bitten on the lip by a horsefly and the pain was so real that when she woke up she examined the spot to see if there were any signs to show that she'd really been bitten.

Chapter 4: EVERY DAY THINGS AND EVENTS

ACCIDENTS

Dreaming about car accidents signifies a reconciliation between relatives and friends, and receiving clothing presents.

BIRTHS

Oddly enough, dreaming about a birth is the sign of an impending death. One afternoon at a party I met an old friend who told me he'd just dreamed that his sister had had a baby. He thought that this might have meant that she was pregnant, and hadn't told him yet, but instead when he returned home, he was greeted with the terrible news that his sister was dead.

Another time, I was at an outdoor party on a stiflingly hot July day and was speaking about dreams, when another party goer said, "I'm afraid your interpretation of birth dreams is correct. A woman once told my wife that she'd dreamed she'd given birth to a beautiful boy whose eyes had separate colors. Just two days later, the woman who'd told her died in a car accident."

BALLOONS

Dreaming about airplanes or balloons is a sign of surprises of all sorts, and also trouble with the eyes and ears.

BRIDGES

Dreaming about crossing over or standing on a bridge signifies a change in one's life routine, such as moving from one house or city to another, or changing one's job or occupation. It can also be a sign of sorrow, usually due to the loss of a friend.

VIVID COLORS IN DREAMS

Without going into detail about the variety of shades of color, color in dreams, especially when it's vivid and predominant, has a great deal of significance. Here are the meanings of each color in a dream:

Light blue signifies upcoming trouble, particularly marriage or domestic troubles, serious disagreements between husband and wife and parents and children. It's also a sign of suicide and murder.

Dark blue: recovery from an illness, reconciliation in a marriage, or reconciliation of relatives and friends, and gifts of animals.

Brown: work and business success.

Black: death and illness.

Green: success in artistic realms; also, a visit or premonition of the occult.

Gold: success in business, investments and romance.

Grey: trouble and danger from an unsuspected source.

Mauve: death and violent catastrophe, often with regard to sight.
Orange: illness or treachery.

Pink: wedding, or an engagements.

Purple: accidents, especially on land.

Red: quarrels, travel, great changes; and accidents, especially by fire.

Violet: success in the arts -- in painting, music, or literature.

Yellow: betrayal by a friend; acts of jealousy and ingratitude.

White, deaths.

Here are some examples. A woman who is extremely psychic dreamed - just prior to her husband's death - that the bedroom became black, and a huge black lobster descended from the ceiling and settled on her.

Another woman, a writer I met through literary contacts, just before her first book manuscript was accepted, dreamed that on her right hand, all of her fingers had rings set with enormous emeralds, and that sun, moon, and sky were all of the brightest and most intense green.

Just before going on a surprise trip to Europe, I met a man who dreamed a red tie fell from the sky and fell at his feet. When he reached down to pick it up, each of his knuckles shined with a bright scarlet glow.

Finally, a woman I know well as a child dreamed she saw a boy walking in front of her with bright yellow hair, and dressed from head to foot in bright yellow clothes. Shortly after this dream, this woman was seriously betrayed by a woman she'd always thought of as a friend.

DANCING

Dreaming about dancing with someone in particular means that person is thinking about doing you harm. If your dancing partner is someone you love, then the dream is telling you that he, or she, is inconstant, and has - at the least! - been flirting with someone else.

If you dream you are dancing by yourself, or are just a spectator at a dance, or you are dancing in a crowd of complete strangers, or with a stranger, then the dream indicates upcoming trouble, often trouble of a petty, domestic kind.

DEATHS, CORPSES AND FUNERALS

Dreaming about a corpse, a death, or a funeral means that you will hear of a birth, an engagement, or a marriage, but not necessarily of the person you're dreaming about.

Sometimes, the dream is literally fulfilled, and the person you're dreaming about dies. I remember dreaming that I went into the dining room of a house where I was staying, and saw a coffin on a table. I was terrified by such a terrible sight, and would have run out of the room at once, but was so curious that I had to go up to the casket and look in. My terror in the dream was made even worse when I realized that the body was that of the friend I was staying with, his face made ugly by advanced decomposition. But the terror became worse because as I stared at the body, the corpse slowly opened its eyes, winked, and stared at me. I woke up sweating with fright, and my host died two days later from a sudden and unexpected heart attack.

A friend of mine, before her brother died, dreamed that she went to the window of her bedroom on a quiet and moonless night. Looking out, she saw her brother standing in a flower garden there, looking up at her. His eyes were blank, his face pale white, and he was wrapped all over in a white sheet. She was so shocked that she woke up and in a few days, got a call that her brother had suddenly died. But these are exceptions, and as a rule, dreams of the dead are usually about good news, of births, engagements, and marriages.

DIGGING
Dreaming about digging is a sign of illness, and sometimes the death, of the one dreaming. Dreaming about seeing someone else digging also signifies an illness or death, but not necessarily that of the digger.

DRESS
Dreaming about a wedding dress is usually a sign of a death, but not necessarily the death of the one wearing the dress. Dreaming about clothes in

general is a sign of petty disappointments and minor illness.

DRINKING

Have you had a dream about drinking (alcohol or otherwise)? That's usually a sign of a visit to some place of entertainment - think amusement parks, movies, etc.

DROWNING

Dreaming about drowning is usually a warning of domestic or financial trouble for the dreamer. Seeing someone else drowning is portends misfortune, either from an accident (sometimes drowning, as seen in the dream), sickness, financial problems, but not always for the drowning person.

Drowning is a common theme in dreams. I've had dreams of friends struggling in a deep pool of water, or a river. In the dream, I've jumped in trying to rescue them, but it was always too late, and sinking deep down into the water, I've come to their cold, clammy corpse. Recently, I dreamed that a close friend fell screaming into a bubbling pool of muddy water. In agony, I tried to rescue him, but was held back by one of those cruel, invisible forces that sometimes haunt dreams. I struggled desperately, but could do no good and while watching my friend, saw his eyes slowly upturn, and the color go from his cheeks. I saw him clutch and unclutch his fingers, throwing them above his head, clawing the air, and finally, he sank into the water with a final, blood-curdling scream for help that rang in my brain as I woke up.

The next day, I got an email from another friend who told me that the friend I'd dreamed about was in terrible trouble because of a sudden illness of his youngest child. The illness was probably incurable, and would likely leave the child a cripple for life.

I've often dreamed that I was drowning myself. I've lived in New York, and dreamed that I was drowning in the East River. In the dreams, I've usually been struggling in the water. Bystanders watched me in horror, but their arms were tied.

Could anything else be more painfully, terribly realistic? The cold, grey stones on the side of the water, and the water flowing swiftly around me. A sensation of falling, having trouble breathing because of the cold, windy air, and then the ice cold sensation of the water. And after every dream of this type, I've experienced trouble, every time.

EATING

Dreaming about eating usually signifies an upcoming accident to the teeth - and a visit to the dentist!

FALLING

Dreaming about falling tells us of an unexpected visit, or an interruption in your daily routine. Who hasn't dreamed of falling, or stepping over the edge of a high precipice, followed by the sickly, terrifying sensation of plunging down until, instead of experiencing the seemingly inevitable final crash, one awakens. This breaking off of the end of this dream is so ordinary that most people think that you can't actually arrive at the bottom in such a dream. However, I've had an experience to the contrary myself, which convinced me that the belief is in error.

FINDING THINGS

Picking up money in a dream usually foretells upcoming petty troubles. How often have many of us in our dreams seen a $100 bill on the street, and after greedily picking it up, seen another, and then others, until the whole street seemed paved with gold. And how bitterly disappointed, I suspect, have we been on waking up to find that our new-found riches had flown away.

Finding a coffin in a dream foretells a death, usually that of a child. Finding bones presages illness or death.

FLOWERS

Since each particular flower, fruit, tree, and vegetable in dreams has a particular meaning, and to deal with all of them would require volumes, I'll have to admit to having limited space, and deal the general outlines of this dream.

But speaking as briefly as possible, in my experience, to dream of:

Buttercups portends presents and kisses.

Carnations, weddings.

Morning glory, an enemy, scheming.
Cornflowers, success in courtship and work.

Cowslips, petty troubles.

Daisies, births.

Daffodils, unfaithful lovers.

Dandelions, illness and minor worries.

Ferns, a sign of a journey.

Foxgloves, a present.

Honeysuckle, deceit on the part of a friend.

Ivy, weddings, friendly actions.

Lilies, engagements, also deaths.

Mignonnette, sorry at a loss of a friend.

Pansies, success in any form of art.

Poppies, breaking off an engagement, or work or business losses.

Primroses, new friendships.

White roses, success in love and the arts.

Yellow roses, danger from deception and jealousy.

Pink roses, engagement, pleasure trips, presents.

Red roses, weddings and inheritances, falling in love.

Sunflowers, land accidents.

Sweet peas, reunions of lost friends and lovers, and kisses.

Tulips, deaths, journeys to foreign countries.

Wallflowers, visits from old friends, and visits to old places.

Forget-me-nots, portends visits and presents from old friends, new clothes, success in work.

Heliotrope, falling in love, visits to fairs and amusement parks, meetings with someone likely to be influential to you.

Violets, reciprocation of affection, presents from lovers. If a girl dreams she's been given a bunch of violets by her love, it's a sure thing that his claims of love are sincere.

KISSES

To dream of being kissed by any particular individual means that the person is not to be trusted. If a girl dreams she's being kissed by her lover, it's a sign that he is not to be trusted.

TREES

The alder tree in a dream is a sign of travel, usually
overseas travel, as well at unrest at home, in life,
and at work.

Ash, bad news of all sorts.

Banyan, traveling and surprises.

Beech, loss of affection (or going away) of friends ;
disappointments in general.

Birch, success at work.

Broom, illness, sometimes death.

Brambles, troubles, both domestic and financial.

Cedar, presents of all kinds ; the loss (by death) of
old friends.

Chestnut, success in love and relationships, falling in love.

Clematis, reunion of old friends and lovers.

Elm, death of relatives, of old friends ; or loss of employment.

Hawthorn, sickness.

Hazel, success of an extraordinary nature; recovery from illness ; escape from accidents.

Lilac, new clothes; present from lover; unexpected invitations.

Mistletoe, great success in relationships and the arts.

Olive, falling in love; the forming of new friendships.

Palm, success in work and rise in social life.

Pine, death, illness ; and a journey to foreign countries.

Poplar, danger from drowning or falling.

Willow, death of a close friend or near relative ; and sorrow due to illness.

Holly, portends illness and trouble.

FRUIT AND VEGETABLES

Dreaming of ....

Apples, portends quarrels.

Beans, presents.

Cabbages, petty losses.

Carrots, new dresses and clothes.

Cherries, presents and kisses.

Gooseberries, domestic quarrels, legal battles.

Grapes, broken friendships.

Pears, births.

Plums, minor accidents.

Wheat, success in work, business and professional life.

Grass, illness, broken engagements, disappointments in general.

Barley and oats, traveling and unexpected visits.

Hay, weddings, vacations, and inheritances.

FIRES

Dreaming about fire sometimes forecasts a fire, and sometimes danger from drowning, also financial difficulties and legal disputes.

FLYING

A flying dream is more common to individuals with psychic abilities and artistic bents than to others. I've asked many artists and writers about this, and they often dream they're flying, but seldom, if ever, with wings. I know the sensation well, for I experience such dreams a lot. Maybe, as I'm walking down a road, I suddenly feel like I can fly. I jump, and the next moment, I'm moving through the air, a yard or so from the ground, with both feet close together. It's an enjoyable sensation, I'm so entranced that I keep telling myself, "It's real this time. I'm not dreaming. I can fly at last." I sometimes see myself in a room full of people, who naturally start laughing when I say I can fly. To show them, I climb on to a table or chair, jump off, and with both feet together, rise to the ceiling, to my own gratification, and the delight of those I'm with. But I feel bitter when I wake up and discover I'm no closer to flying than before.

Many times I've dreamed I was in a huge, empty house, being chased by some monster. After being chased up staircases and along blood-curdling corridors, I'm finally cornered in a gloomy top attic. Everything seems hopeless and I'm expecting to be caught every second, when just as the monster bounds into the room, I jump on a window sill and with a mighty bounce, spring up into space. And then, with great joy, instead of falling, I find that I can fly far away into the distant sky where there's nothing to stop me.

I've kept a careful count of the number of flying dreams I've had in the last year, and they amounted to eighteen. That's a fairly high percentage! What happens after them? Generally a surprise visit, an unexpected journey or communication, or abnormally heavy correspondence, nothing more serious. But as far as dreams go, I know of few that are more fascinating than these.

INSANITY

Dreaming about insanity is a sign of impending troubles of all kinds. Often the dream is, to a large extent, fulfilled. I remember a woman saying to me once, "I dreamed last night that my brother and I were sitting by ourselves eating breakfast, when something made me suddenly look up at him, and I saw an odd glitter in his eyes, a look that made my blood run cold. He soon made frightening grimace, showing his teeth, bulging out his eyes, and frowning, and his features were contorted like they were made of rubber. I felt a shiver of almost unspeakable terror, knowing there was real evil with me, and I jumped up and ran for the door, and as I did, he laughed loudly, and chased after me screaming, 'I'm crazy! I'm crazy! I'm going to chop you to pieces.'"

I woke up terribly afraid, just as (in the dream) he had caught me by my hair and was going to kill me. Within a week, he was hospitalized with an insane dementia.

MARRIAGE

Dreaming about marriage often signifies death or illness, but not necessarily of the bride or bridegroom.

MOON

Dreaming about the moon is usually a sign of illness, usually a mental illness, but not necessarily that of the dreamer; also domestic or financial problems, and death by drowning.

While in Chicago a few years ago, I mentioned a boating death that had recently occurred there to a local sportsman, who exclaimed, "I knew something of that sort would happen, because I dreamed about the moon two nights in a row," and he went on to explain that whenever he had such dreams, somebody was sure to drown nearby.

MONEY

Dreaming about picking up money, as I mentioned already, signifies petty troubles. Dreams about seeing money, minor illnesses and surprise visits.

MURDER

Dreaming about being murdered portends domestic troubles, and troubles with neighbors and losing things. Dreaming that another person is murdered signifies great danger to that person.

For instance, I've been told of a woman who had a vivid dream that she saw someone enter her aunt's room, while her aunt was asleep, and smother her with a pillow. Everything was completely realistic: the door opening slowly, the pasty-faced, evil-eyed intruder with a flashlight, the intruder's big knuckles and broken nails; the expression of evil in her eyes as she lifted the pillow and her quick movement as she brought it down on the sleeping aunt's face; the tightening of her lips, and the straightening of her bare arms as she pressed on the victim with all of her weight; the kicking of the bedclothes, at first frantic, and then weaker and weaker, finally stopping altogether with a tiny tug of the sheet as the sleeper woke up. It was all terrible and very graphic. A few days later, she got an unexpected call that her aunt had been robbed and murdered in a hotel while traveling in Europe.

THE NAKED-DREAM

Almost everyone has had the experience of dreaming themselves naked in a public place, with a crowd staring at them. A dream of this type happened to someone I know, who is a well-known public figure. He dreamed that he and his brother were walking in a public area in their area, and he suddenly noticed that everyone around was staring at them in a very odd way. Wondering what it meant, he checked to make sure that his clothes were OK, and realized that he and his brother were both completely naked. Terrified, he grabbed his brother's arm and whispered to him, "Get the first cab you see! And don't stop to ask any questions!" His brother shook him off and kept walking, and started greeting others he passed on the way. A small child screamed out, saying, "Look! Look! They have nothing on!" At that point, a cop ran across the street and hustled the two brothers into a waiting police van, as a huge crowd stared at them.

The man couldn't remember what happened after that, but woke up frightened, but the dream in reality seemed to foretell good fortune because he received an unexpected and good promotion in his job.

My own experience of a naked dream was very similar. In the dream, I went to an important costume party dressed, or so I thought, in a fantastic, complete costume from the middle ages. When I walked in, I was surprised that everyone stopped dancing and stared at me. Feeling very flattered, I was walking across the room to one of the only available seats, when one of the hosts, his face red with fury, came up to me quickly, and in a voice quivering with rage, said, "How dare you show up like this?" I was completely surprised by his response to my costume, and responded that I thought my outfit was very ordinary. "Ordinary?," he yelled, "Look at yourself," and when I looked in the mirror, I was shocked to see that I had nothing on. "Catch him," the host screamed, and suddenly all the guests, armed with chairs, rushed after me, but fortunately, I was still a few feet ahead of my pursuers when I woke up.

Another time, I dreamed I was passing the offering plate in a big church, when all the men turned and scowled at me. Unable to imagine what I had done wrong, I was about to sneak away as fast as I could when the usher tapped me on the shoulder, whispering, "What happened to your clothes? You had them on a minute ago." And I was horrified to realize that my clothes were all gone, and I was completely naked. I cried out as I dropped the offering plate, and woke up. After each of these dreams, I had an unexpected success in my work.

From what I've been told, it's usually the more modest people who have this sort of dream. I remember a man seated next to me once on a flight across the Pacific. He was a conservative minister, a mild and respectable man. Respectable, that is, in every area but his dreams. When he found out my interest in dreams, he proceeded to tell me for several hours in great detail about his unusual - for him - dreams. And I think he was enjoying the lurid details.

"Last night," he recounted, "I dreamed that I'd visited a family in my congregation. These are very good people, faithful and respected, but in the dream, we were sitting and talking when their daughter Martha - home from college for spring break - walked in the room stark naked. Her mother was shocked, and screamed at her, 'Martha, what's the matter with you? Are you crazy?' But before she'd finished speaking, she ran from the room, and I realized that I, too, had no clothes on."

Dreams of this sort are generally good signs, and should be welcomed.

PEOPLE OF CERTAIN PROFESSIONS OR TRADES

Dreaming of an actor or actress portends success in love.

An author, a reunion with an old friend.

A chef or baker, missing a plane flight.

A contractor, a gift in the form of clothing.

A clergyman, sharp pain or an upset stomach.

An airline pilot, an injury to the head.

A pharmacist, getting into debt.

A farmer, an accident involving injury to the feet or legs.

A manager (especially of a grocery store), sickness.

A dentist, illness or death.

A dress designer, kisses.

A doctor, danger from wild animals.

A lawyer, financial losses and danger from dog bites.

A nail technician, presents from someone who loves you, or success in love.

A publisher, danger from stinging insects.

A politician, a birth.

A sailor, a household accident.

A soldier, breaking glass or china.
A tailor, quarrels with your in-laws.

A beggar, a present of a dog or cat.

An undertaker, an accident endangering your teeth.

PRESENTS

Dreaming of presents signifies insignificant
financial losses

SLEEP

To dream that you are asleep foretells a visit from or to an old friend.

THE SUN

Dreaming about the sun is a sign of upcoming success in business and distinction in work.

STONES AND METALS -- PRECIOUS AND OTHERWISE

Amethyst, success in love.

Bloodstones, inheritances.

Coral, a birth.

Cornelian, betrayal.

Diamonds, drowning.

Emeralds, great success in the arts.

Jasper, unreliability.

Opal, separation, divorce, breaks in friendships.

Pearls, great sorrow.

Rubies, kisses of a lover.

Turquoise, breaking an engagement.

Sapphires, a wedding.

Pebbles, petty troubles.

Black rocks, illness and death.

Sand, a serious accident.

Chalk, an illness or death of a child.

Granite, a land accident.

Marble, death.

TEETH

Dreaming about teeth is a sign of illness or death, but not necessarily that of the dreamer. A man told me, for example, that on the night preceding the death of one of his brothers, he dreamed that his teeth fell out, and that on one of them was a portrait of the brother who died.

TRAVELING

Dreaming about boat travel, cruising or airline flights signifies unexpected news, an invitation or a visit from a stranger. Dreaming about land travel is a sign of minor worries and losses.

Who hasn't dreamed about rushing to an airport and missing a plane or getting on the wrong plane without the chance to get off? Or getting on a plane without a ticket or without one's traveling companion or without luggage, or of seeing friends getting on the wrong plane, and they themselves stranded in a strange and unfamiliar place. Almost everything goes wrong in traveling in dreamland and we wake up with our brains in a swirl, conscious only that we are lost, and fearing we'll never see our relatives or home again.

Almost everyone has had this kind of dream. Another variation of these dreams are of shipwrecks or plane crashes. Oddly enough, if someone dreams of their cruise ship sinking, it's usually a sign of a land accident, often a minor or trivial one. But dreaming of a plane crash is usually a sign of danger on the water or from other sources.

SUICIDE

Dreaming about suicide usually portends illness and troubles of all kinds. Dreaming about someone else committing suicide also signifies illness and trouble.

WATER

Dreaming about clear water portends good luck of various kinds and the end of trouble.

Dreaming about muddy water is a sign of illness, death, and troubles of all varieties.

WEATHER

Dreaming about the wind signifies quarrels, making enemies and troubles in love and marriage.

Dreaming about rain portends tears.

Snow and ice, illness or death.

Sunshine, success in love, good inheritances, and presents.

THE HODGEPODGE DREAM

Dreams that fly from one scene to another with breathtaking speed and the characters are mixed and everything is hopelessly mixed up seem to be meaningless, but they often contain significant features.

This is an example. A certain doctor dreamed he was riding a bicycle through a park one sunny morning, when a woman dressed all in pink and yellow pushed a baby carriage straight in front of him, and he was thrown head over heels off the bike. But instead of hitting the ground, he found himself running around in a cage at the local zoo with nothing on. Then, just as his mother-in-law, her face bright red with rage rushed at him with an umbrella open, the scene changed, and he was picking up coins in the street as fast as he could. One of the coins, as he was about to drop it in his

pocket turned into a friend of his, who in turn
forced him under a pump, and made him drink
until he could drink no more. The friend then took
a gun, and swore that unless our doctor continued
drinking, he would shoot. At that point, the
unfortunate dreamer was about to try and force
more water down his throat when the fountain
suddenly became a car and he found himself
desperately trying to join his wife who was sitting
down but was in danger of being crushed by a huge
baby sitting on the roof of the car, and the roof was
too weak to support the baby's weight. The man
was in agony and seemed unable to save his wife,
and as he tried to jump on top of the car to move
the baby off, a cop grabbed him, threw him off the
car and he saw the roof give way, the baby fall in,
and his wife was crushed. Then swearing and
screaming , he tumbled backwards and found
himself in his own home where he found his wife
flirting with someone he hated. Screaming in
anger, he grabbed a sword and cut off both of their
heads, and realized to his horror that far from
being the two people he thought, they were two of

his patients. While he was desperately trying to
decide what to do, the door burst open and his wife
and all of her relatives ran in and accused him,
followed by the police, and he was executed the
next morning.

In this dream, crazy as it sounds, there are many
significant items. Sunshine denotes success in love,
the woman's pink and yellow dress, a wedding and
treachery. The accident, reconciliation; running
naked, success in work; his mother-in-law's red
face, success in the arts. Picking up money, petty
troubles; water (clear), end of troubles and good
luck again; the car, a visit from a stranger and
unexpected news. Accident to his wife, trouble with
an inheritance. Kisses, unfaithfulness. Murder,
domestic troubles. Execution, divorce.

All of these signs were verified. Shortly after the
dream, our doctor proposed to a woman and was
accepted. The wedding took place quickly, and
almost immediately after, the couple fought over a
comment made to the doctor by one of his wife's

friends. Reconciliation took place quickly, at almost the same time that he had been hired in a good position. There were a number of disagreements between the two. His wife's artistic temperament not always working well with her husband who was more matter-of-fact and practical. Then there was another brief spell of happiness. The husband got back in touch with a cousin whom he hadn't seen in years and the day his cousin left, his father became deathly sick. His father left the bulk of his will to a stranger who had had a bad influence over him, an influence that unfortunately couldn't be legally proved. The disappointment over the will led to further troubles with his wife whose repeated affairs left him with no alternative but to divorce her. Now, since all of these things happened so rapidly, it's clear to me that a hodgepodge dream may mean much that is tragic will come to pass.

SUMMARY FOR LOVERS

To dream that the one you love is clothed in light blue or yellow signifies they are fickle.

In dark blue or gold, that they are faithful.

To present or receive from the object of one's affections, or to see him or her wearing a yellow rose, poppy or daffodil means that he or she is unfaithful.

On the other hand, if in the place of those flowers are buttercups, white roses, or sweet peas, it means he or she is faithful.

To dream one is kissing one's sweetheart signifies unfaithfulness on the part of the dreamer.

To dream that one sees one's sweetheart kissing, or being kissed by someone else, is a sign of unfaithfulness of the one dreamed about.
To dream about dancing with the object of one's affection means that the latter is, or will be, guilty of flirting with someone else.

To dream of the object of one's affections in connection with ash or beech trees, grass, crows, owls, tortoiseshell cats, spaniels, eels, black horses, moths, monkey, wasps, tigers, wolves, and hanging, is a sign of fickleness and unfaithfulness on the loved one's part, which not infrequently leads to a breaking off of an engagement, and in cases of marriage, to separation and divorce.

To dream of one's beloved one in connection with cherries, ducks and gnats portends kisses from him or her.

To dream of him or her in connection with cedars, lilacs, pigeons, and ladybirds portends presents.

To dream of him or her in connection with black cats, silver foxes, grey horses, bees, worms, and lions signifies he or she is faithful, that the engagement will lead to marriage, and that the latter will prove in every way happy.

FINISHING UP - YOU AND YOUR DREAMS

In the end, you're doing to dream every time you sleep. Finding out what your dreams mean can be a helpful and good thing, and realizing their meanings will give you a peace about them - even when the meanings aren't necessarily good.

Everyone dreams, but most people are not systematic about their dreams, and that's what I'd encourage for you. Here are some suggestions to make the most of your dreams.

1. Write them down. Making notes about your dreams will help you remember them and make sense of them. I'd suggest you keep a pad and pen by your bed so that you can make notes as soon as you wake up. If you wake up during the night with a dream that's particularly disturbing, it's not a bad idea to make some notes then and there. Even the

act of writing them down will help you sort out even the most disturbing of dreams.

2. Talk about your dreams. If you're married and your husband or wife will talk about them, that's probably the best. But if not a spouse, then a friend who will hear your dreams and offer suggestions is the next best thing. (It goes without saying that you can also listen to - and offer ideas about) their dreams, too.

3. A really disturbing or frightening dream might need to be discussed with a professional. If you're in any type of therapy, sharing your dreams will probably help your therapist to understand the issues you're dealing with. But even an occasional listening ear from an objective third party (such as your doctor or minister) can be helpful.

4. There are lots of online forums dealing with dreams, and a lot of the folks there are ready to help, and are good at helping you. Using those

forums and other online helps is something you should make use of.

5. Finally, don't let a fear of dreams ruin your sleep. Accept the reality that you're going to dream, and know that your dreams are often a way of understanding and gaining insight into your waking life. Welcome that insight, and know that it's a good thing. Happy dreams!

Printed in Great Britain
by Amazon

37922770R00057